GAMING

GAMING

The Fine Art of Creating Simulation/Learning Games for Religious Education

Dennis Benson

abingdon audio·graphics
Nashville

GAMING: THE FINE ART OF CREATING
SIMULATION/LEARNING GAMES FOR RELIGIOUS EDUCATION

Copyright © 1971 by Dennis Benson

All rights in this book are reserved. No part of the book may be reproduced in any manner whatsoever without written permission of the publishers except brief quotations embodied in critical articles or reviews. For information address Abingdon, Nashville, Tennessee

ISBN 0-687-13995-3

Scripture quotations unless otherwise noted are from the Revised Standard Version of the Bible, copyrighted 1946 and 1952 by the Division of Christian Education, National Council of Churches, and are used by permission.

MANUFACTURED BY THE
PARTHENON PRESS, NASHVILLE, TENNESSEE,
UNITED STATES OF AMERICA

Contents

GAMBIT ONE	Playmates	**7**
GAMBIT TWO	What's Happening in the Sandbox?	**9**
GAMBIT THREE	Foreplay	**10**
GAMBIT FOUR	"What's a nice faith like you doing in a place like this?"	**13**
GAMBIT FIVE	RALPH	**16**
GAMBIT SIX	BLIND	**21**
GAMBIT SEVEN	BREAD	**28**
GAMBIT EIGHT	FLIGHT 108	**31**
GAMBIT NINE	FIG LEAF AND EAST OF EDEN	**35**
GAMBIT TEN	CRUNCH	**38**
GAMBIT ELEVEN	MIND FLINTS	**56**
GAMBIT TWELVE	PLAYMANSHIP	**61**

Contents

GAMBIT ONE   Playmates   **7**
GAMBIT TWO   What's Happening in the Sandbox?   **9**
GAMBIT THREE   Foreplay   **10**
GAMBIT FOUR   "What's a nice faith like you doing in a place like this?"   **13**
GAMBIT FIVE   RALPH   **16**
GAMBIT SIX   BLIND   **21**
GAMBIT SEVEN   BREAD   **28**
GAMBIT EIGHT   FLIGHT 108   **31**
GAMBIT NINE   FIG LEAF AND EAST OF EDEN   **35**
GAMBIT TEN   CRUNCH   **38**
GAMBIT ELEVEN   MIND FLINTS   **56**
GAMBIT TWELVE   PLAYMANSHIP   **61**

GAMBIT ONE:

Playmates

Many folk have given of themselves to create the games shared in this book. They have bravely risked with me as we exposed their people to the results of our common planning. My thanks to the following creative co-creators: Kenneth Haines, Chris Scott, Dave Warner, Elmer Reamer (the voice of Ralph), educator Dr. Howard Robertson, Maxine North, Lynn Bracy, Glenn Engel, Philip Britton, Gregory Smith, Jane Mall, Bob Beams, Helsel Marsh, Dorothy Wagenhorst, Jim Long, Ray De Vries, Jim Walthers, Roger Boekenhauer, Jeff Sell, Thisbe Watkins, Joan Sherman, Marge De Vries, Linda MacConnel, Sue Mathias, Warren Bulette, Sam Ruta, Toni Ruta, James Davis, and many other unnamed brothers and sisters.

A number of local churches and church conferences have boldly let me and their folk explore in the realm of gaming. I am deeply appreciative to them for this kind of freedom. It is good to be part of the creative church.

My playful family (Marilyn, Jill, and Amy) have pulled me into more simulation/stimulation games than I would have ever experienced alone. We are going to play a lot more as we learn together. It has been very good.

Betsy McClure whipped all of this into typescript with minimum time and maximum care.

GAMBIT TWO:

What's happening in the sandbox?

LISTEN TO RECORD 1, SIDE 1, BANDS 1 AND 2!

GAMBIT THREE:

Foreplay

This is a disposable book. It is created to enable you to do without it. The next few minutes of print and sound are designed to help you rediscover something that only *you* can do well with your people: learning through playing.

A fad is sweeping the land. Every publisher and producer is offering teachers boxes filled with things they call simulation games. It is a strange kind of fad. It's strange because even the experts don't really know what happens when a person plays a simulation game. Is it just an extension of role playing? Is it matched role playing? The studies on how much cognitive experience the student picks up are pretty sketchy. This print/sound experience challenges the value implicit in packaged games. I don't think that the game's the thing. I am hunching that it is the creation of play that makes learning exciting.

I vividly remember hours of walking from my home to school. When alone, I would boldly give great speeches to imaginary throngs. I'd urge vast masses to undertake impossible tasks.

I'd pacify angry crowds. Beautiful maidens would be moved to tears and love. I'd humbly accept great honors from the powers of the world. I was verbally and emotionally playing a fantasy game. I was, in a sense, rehearsing what I hoped would become reality. Unfortunately (or fortunately) most of the situations that I played at when I was a strolling youngster have never come true. However, it's amazing how these moments of game playing come flashing back to my mind when I am called to play a reality game with contemporary situations.

Most of our people have enjoyed playing at the task of learning. How many American capitalists first learned to accumulate wealth by playing Monopoly on the floor of their living room? Many clergymen, statesmen, and fast-talk artists perfected their skills by role playing these particular identities when they were just children. Even now, my five-year-old whips up the most fantastic meals for me at her imaginary stove. She is learning for the future through

GAMBIT THREE FOREPLAY

playing. Such educational playing is in the life experience of our constituents.

Theological man in every age has played games concerning the present and future. The frightened passengers traveling with the fleeing Jonah could play at casting lots to learn what was happening to them. The soldiers at the foot of the Cross played a game of dice to discover how to divide the dying man's few possessions. Jesus noted the contrast between the playing of those who criticized him and children playing games of weddings and funerals (Matt. 11:16-17). Today some people give a religious mystique to the drawing of special game cards as they try to discover what life will give them.

All of us play various games as part of our immediate experience. We play for different reasons and different stakes. A girl may play the game of love. She wants a man. A man may play the game of the company. The promotion is his prize. A parent may play the game of manipulation. He seeks the control of his teenager. Some people even play the game of war and death.

Many of these games are played with words. We say things we do not mean. We communicate things that are not reality. We use words to keep emotions masked and hidden. We construct beautiful word games or fences to keep people away from us. Words can become a means by which we protect our inner emotions from the world. The late Eric Berne (*Games People Play* [New York: Grove Press, 1970]) has enabled us to see only too clearly the kinds of word games that fill our daily lives. Perhaps it is this kind of verbal play experience in all of us that makes us strangely attracted to the idea of learning through playing games.

What follows in this short print/sound experience is the excitement, the froth of doing and creating games of learning. Instead of just packaging things for you to take out of a box we are choosing a different path. This book is going to share with you the kinds of games my friends and I have been creating for the past several years. These games have been created in ordinary situations by people who have gotten themselves together around challenging teaching tasks. In most cases, the people who created these games had never played learning games before. They were simply people who had been enabled to tie together mutual strengths, particular goals, and the energies of their people. The result of this mixture has been authentic learning experience. The joy and fun of our discovering are our real gifts to you.

It is important that you remember this kind of origin. Some of my friends are taking simulation games in education very seriously. I recently was visited by one such colleague. He wanted my counsel on how his research group could set up a complete video tape operation whereby each person playing a game could be taped. He wanted to explore an operation which would focus a different camera on each participant. His research group would then carefully analyze each aspect of the event in order to determine scientifically just what was going on. They have been spending years researching just what is happening when students use games to learn. Brothers and sisters, don't look to this print/sound experience for this kind of research. We are not probing *why* these

GAMING

learning ventures authentically happened. Not long ago I spent some time with two psychologists. I confessed to my friends that little formal research was part of my experimentation. They probed the scope and nature of the experiences with games I have had across the country. They soothed my concern about the lack of the research dimension of my work. I was urged to keep doing real teaching probes with people in various contexts. They suggested that too many people get mired in the research slough and are never able to transport "studies" to teachers and students in learning situations.

Well, my folk and I are passing along to you what we have done. This is a book that is created to enable you to play learning games with your people as your situation dictates. You will quickly gain confidence by realizing that you can create games as good (or better) than those created by the folk in the book. You will then be on your own. You won't need this book, nor will you need any boxed games. You'll be free to do something authentic on your own.

Brothers and sisters, be free and enjoy learning. There is a lot of fun and excitement ahead for you and your people.

GAMBIT FOUR:

"What's a nice faith like you doing in a place like this?"

I get uptight when I face something unfamiliar. I really do. I experience some anxiety when I first listen to a new LP by a favorite rock group when I know that it represents a change in style. Even that wild recent flick with a new style brings a bit of discomfort to me at first. A crazy new food that I've not eaten before raises suspicions in my mind.

Most of us have feelings like these when we come to matters religious. We somehow like to have the content of faith take a familiar form. We don't have to be ashamed of this desire. The important thing is that we aren't panicked by fear when we encounter innovation in faith expression. This is just the natural discomfort experienced whenever a new wineskin is filled with our basic message. It is significant that we recognize the source of our discomfort. There is a great temptation for us to mask our feelings in suspicion and anger. Immediately we want to put a value judgment on that which doesn't quite look like it did yesterday. We emotionally demand to have the holy taste, feel, and smell a certain way. It should be the same today and tomorrow as it was yesterday.

We are particularly rigid when we come to the task of learning religion. We have been conditioned to expect that the religious content dictates a narrow and stiff teaching style. We look at the message and it seems awesome in most religious contexts. Therefore, religious education must also be awesome. This limiting mindset is cast from the forms in which we preserve our faith. Religion is usually stored in rows and rows of words. Print is formal and set. Religion comes from the mouths of people with straight faces and stiff necks. Religion is ritualistically celebrated in pious, solemn buildings and sanctuaries. However, this stately order is deadly in contrast to the excitement of the religious content and the electric age. The center of the faith content is explosive by its very nature. The electric life around us bristles with vitality. Teachers often deny the buzz of our age and surrender to educational forms which are just a cultural mindset from the recent past.

GAMING

Religious teaching often entombs a living faith in morbid teaching styles.

We are living in an electronic environment. Christ has somehow come forth into a setting that is filled no longer with sheep and scrolls. We suddenly are alive in an age smeared by jets and transistors. We can long for yesterday. However, God only gives us today in which to be and do the truth with our brothers and sisters. At the same time, we secretly know that tomorrow is already here. It is hard to superimpose the simple shepherd on the age of the printed circuit.

All our input comes to us in a way that demands participation. The television set reaches out to massage and caress our minds. The electric media touch us as they seek to sell and tell us something. They want to move us. They want to convince us. They are playing with our minds.

There is no way to escape this electronic web. The time ahead promises more complex and complete electric input. We will be simply overloaded by the flood of vibrations moving through our nerve endings. What is a nice faith like you doing in a place like this? I guess that we really can't answer that question. However, it is important to do something about the content, the essence of what we are doing here. Man, who comes from a theological base, has a content related to history. His capacity to communicate his content and his history are seriously challenged by the electronic age. He must make a stand in the electric environment in order to give his faith flesh.

One of the most underachieved aspects of human existence is play. We have a hard time really living with play. We like to say that we are really a fantastically fun-loving culture. We may even know that we need more play in our lives. However, most of us know that we secretly have a difficult time struggling with leisure time. We all long for more time. More time for what? Maybe it is fun to get at the lawn or complete that do-it-yourself project. Perhaps we get a real buzz out of watching television and eating popcorn. One of the great moments of our life may even come when we can go bowling. However, I suspect that we still have to admit that there must be more to celebration and play than this. How do we play?

One style of getting man's need to find the process of finding the theological answer is that of playing learning games. Like so many other communication processes it is still a technique cloaked in mystery with little explanation. It is a great temptation to be overwhelmed by every new learning probe or method. We are ideal candidates for the "centipede trauma." There was once an insect with many legs who tried to ponder the problem of which leg he moved first. He thought and thought. He looked at one leg after another. He decided to move and see which leg responded. He suddenly realized that he wasn't able to move at all. This is not an argument for the lack of rationality or intelligence. There certainly is a place for a probing kind of analysis in every situation. However, there is also a dimension to a task that simply involves doing. The process of finding truth is also the act of being and doing the truth. Playing is one of

GAMBIT FOUR "WHAT'S A NICE FAITH LIKE YOU DOING IN A PLACE LIKE THIS?"

the important ways to seek the meaning of the faith.

By utilizing simulation/stimulation games, we can quickly tap the deep roots that lie within most of our constituents. There is something childlike and primitive that come to the surface in such a learning style. The quality of participation and expectation will replace the customary flat or boring style of theological study experienced in many religious contexts.

However, good learning is more than style. What are your goals? What are you really trying to enable your constituents to do and be? These are simple questions that have jarring implications. If you can answer in a sentence or two without much reflection—be suspicious. You've oversimplified it or you don't understand what you really have said. Learning enablers must continually struggle with these queries. If you do not have some kind of grounding on these questions, you will meet only with frustration after the learning experiences have been completed. You will be forced by default to accept other people's criteria of evaluation for what you are doing. One man's understanding of success may be another's grief. Each particular setting, each particular event, demands its own set of criteria for judgment and evaluation based on its goals. I call this the debriefing process. Perhaps the group should debrief what it has done itself. This pattern will emerge more clearly as we move into the actual game situations in this book.

The probing question of what really has been accomplished should be faced continually. Don't ever lose that point of tension. That's a probing kind of inquiry that you must always seek whenever you teach or enable others to learn. However, we cannot be trapped in uncertainty like the centipede. We must move beyond the question of how we arrived at a certain place. We must simply acknowledge where we are and use any means possible to proceed toward our goal.

The simple gimmick or the fad cannot really resolve the constant tension between new wine and old wineskins. However, there is a way to keep alive in the electronic environment. This means of keeping alive is not simply using the latest audio-visual aid. It is not merely a response that is triggered by some more materials that are dumped into our lap. It is my contention that we keep alive in this constant tension between who we are and where we are by continually fleshing out our message in new and authentic ways. We flesh this message out by getting into the message itself and letting our constituents get into us. It is the "enabler," the teacher, whose task it is to bring together the content and the constituents by all kinds of means. The media or the means by which the wineskin and wine interrelate are vital and changing. There is no one solution to this vast problem. Let's move on to the gaming perspective and not accept the limitation of where we have been.

GAMBIT FIVE: RALPH

The committee of eight people was struggling to find a medium by which some of their people could have a meaningful weekend retreat on communication. Ideas began to stack up. "I remember an old, old story about a scientist who learned that an 'ether' would encompass the earth. He made a special environment which protected him. When the gas had passed the earth, he went out and found all the people lifeless. He was in utter despair until they started to wake up. They had only been sleeping. I think that Sir Arthur Conan Doyle wrote it." The school principal had just finished this mind probe when a young person spoke up. "I was really turned on by *2001: A Space Odyssey*. The fact that a machine could run people's lives and be wrong really got me." The ideas began to stick together. Out of three, two-hour sessions came the game we called, RALPH.

We found ourselves working as taskforce pairs. We also realized that we didn't need a whole weekend. We decided to follow our design in the course of one day. Our goal was simply to facilitate deeper communication between persons as they dealt with a number of social-ethical-theological problems.

STOP READING! PLAY RECORD I, SIDE II, BAND I.

One taskforce pair prepared seven Sunday school rooms for the event. Each room had the windows covered with plain paper. There was a cassette tape recorder and tape placed on the table in each area. A survival kit containing bread, peanut butter, a jar of water, and a few cookies was placed in one corner of the rooms.

Another pair produced a tape recording. The tape was the main thrust of the event. The people gathered on the Saturday of the communication lab and were asked to relax and close their eyes. The first portion of the tape was played. A voice with a background tone spoke in syllables. It identified itself as the voice of a survival computer. The people were invited to know him as "RALPH." He told them that the radiation contamination in the atmosphere had continued to build up until it was now deemed dangerous for humans. The people were then instructed by RALPH to follow appointed guides to the protective environments which had been prepared for them. They would be given more instructions later.

The groups had been divided by armbands as they registered. Each armband bearer went into the prepared rooms according to the color of his band. The first instructions from RALPH were to seal the environment with the radiation shielding substance (masking tape around the door). The next two hours were filled with demanding problems concerning the life of that group of people.

The first challenge involved the use of latecomers. They were to be the survivors who may have been exposed to contamination. Each group was challenged to observe the person inside its environment for so many microchrons (new time unit equaling about one-seventh of a minute). After that time they had either to risk keeping the person (and contamination?) or return him to certain death. The survivors were told to keep silent and act as if they didn't understand the comments and questions of the people in the groups.

The responses of the different groups of players were amazing. One unit of people would not let into their environment the survivor who knocked. They later confessed that they didn't want to get emotionally involved. It was easier for them to keep out a person who might bring in contamination when they didn't have to face him. Another community of players

GAMBIT FIVE RALPH

let the person in, but when the time came for them to make a choice about keeping him, they sent him out to his death. They later explained that he seemed useless to them because he couldn't talk. He wouldn't benefit their community. Those in yet another shelter took the survivor and refused at every point to sacrifice him even for their survival.

In the course of the next three hours each community underwent a series of crises. RALPH'S voice on tape provided their one source of direction. We set the tape recorder in the hall adjoining the six rooms. Many groups recorded the transmissions on their cassette machines in order to have the messages correctly understood. In the course of the game we offered a work break within the protective environment which enabled each group to eat lunch from the survival kit.

I have included a complete recording of RALPH'S voice transmissions in this book. I have foreshortened the recording only by excluding the repetition of the directions. RALPH repeated the instructions twice.

NOW LISTEN TO RECORD II, SIDES I & II, IN ORDER TO FOLLOW THE COMPLETE THRUST OF THE GAME.

After the last task was completed by each group, we moved from the shelters. We were afraid that their kidneys could not hold much longer. The debriefing sessions which followed lasted three hours. I had a hard time moderating it. The people were bursting to talk out this fantastic experience of making ethical decisions under such acute pressure. The survivor who

GAMING

wasn't let into the room struck out emotionally at those who wouldn't take him in. "How did you know who I was? Didn't I have a right to life, too?" Someone cut into the hot discussion with the searing inquiry, "Didn't Jesus tell us to lay down our lives for one another?" (John 15:12-13).

One group had kept everyone within their protective environment and had "faith." They were attacked by the "rational" group. "You can't be emotional and survive. We had to save ourselves!" (Romans 8:35-39). Another group admitted that if they had to choose between the "faith" group and the "rational" group, they would choose the people who used their minds.

Someone asked why there weren't any women in charge of groups. "Why didn't you choose women as your leaders?" The male chauvinism within the group was released. The preconceptions of our society were suddenly seen as having been imposed on this chance to build a new world. The agonizing crunch between faith and human reality was experienced.

The ethical decisions made revealed naked theological positions. How do we bring together how we feel and act with what Christ has made us to be through our baptism and faith? There were awing gaps of artificial responses when this point emerged in the discussion. One man offered his experience as a computer engineer. "All of the hard ethical problems within this game are possible—if not probable." Silence hung in the air.

A young girl confessed that she was near tears when the time came in their group to implement the decision to cast out the survivor that they had taken in earlier in the game. He did not get up and leave. They had to drag him from the room. This was the only way they could solve the problem of removing one person from their overtaxed environment. "Well, why didn't you stop us? Why did you stand and just whimper? Don't you have the nerve to act on the conviction of your faith?" The questions reached out and slapped the comfortable positions of many in the room. How does the Christian act properly in making these kinds of decisions in the technological age?

One of the younger members of the group raised an avenue of inquiry which made the group even more theologically sensitive. "We were actually worshiping the computer! What if RALPH was wrong? Why did we make him our god?" Even the more "rational" responses to the crises had accepted without question RALPH'S infallibility. We had given each group a computer programming card. This was designed as an escape valve in case the pressure became too much for any one person. Any group could use the card to challenge the computer. No one did. They had in fact accepted the control of the machine. RALPH had become their ultimate concern. The room seemed to be filled with the echoing choice set before Israel by Joshua. ("And if you be unwilling to serve the Lord, choose this day whom you will serve" Joshua 24:15.) Are we too far gone to make this kind of choice any longer?

The time just ran out. We then went into another room where a table had been set in a huge circle. In the middle of this community table set for seventy-five people was a loaf

GAMBIT FIVE RALPH

of bread and a pitcher of wine. We ate and let the pressure work down into celebration. Then we celebrated the sacrament of the Eucharist. The final act of the day was the experience of passing the Peace to one another.

NOW PLAY RECORD I, SIDE II, BAND II. IT CONTAINS DEBRIEFING COMMENTS BY THE MEMBERS OF THE PLANNING COMMITTEE.

A Recap of RALPH

GOAL: To enable a group of adults and young people to relate to one another as they struggle with certain social, ethical, and theological problems.

TOOLS:
1. A planning group of 4-8 people.
2. A group of students: adults and young people.
3. Several classrooms which have had the windows covered and are furnished with only a plain table with cassette tape recorder.
4. The record enclosed with this book of RALPH'S instructions, or a tape prepared from that record.
5. A record player or tape recorder which can broadcast the sound to all the adjoining rooms of people.
6. Armbands to divide the main body into sub-groups.
7. Survival bags of food which will provide a cramped, but possible lunch for the group if they share.
8. Computer cards which have been imprinted with RALPH'S number and name to be used by anyone who is uptight about anything. They can write a message and push it out under the door as input to RALPH.
9. Arrangements for food (we had it catered by going to nearby restaurants and bringing it back).

STEPS:
1. Planning of the event by a group of the constitutents.
2. Task force assignments.
3. Preparation in advance of all the needed equipment and meeting areas.
4. Introduction to the group by playing the first part of the tape (or record).
5. After placing the groups in their "protective environments" have them follow the instructions of RALPH.
6. Release them at the end of their isolation and take a break for the use of the bathroom (unless you have adjoining facilities for each group).
7. Debrief for a period of time equal to or longer than the room stay.
8. Love feast and sacramental conclusions.

Do you remember that our style of game playing is that *you* make the design according to your needs and goals? Maybe you will want

19

GAMING

to take this idea in an entirely different direction. You might try to adapt this idea to a one-hour format. Another way I have used this design is for a large youth conference. The three hundred young people were subdivided into the smaller isolated communities in the college classrooms. They only met with a slightly larger group for debriefing. Each participating church was then given a cassette with programmed follow-through material to be taken back to the local church for continuity of experience into the Sunday night group. We paired the young people from the churches. A pair gives security and yet also enables each person to be double covered.

The use of this design has evoked amazing results. The process of playing at such an intensive ethical situation builds up a great deal of involvement within each person. This highly focused experience merges the personal and theological levels of learning. This has been one of the most satisfying game situations I have experienced. Even one of the small sections of this game can be expanded to fit one of your particular focuses.

Be very free to experiment with RALPH. You can preselect the bands (Record II) which contain the particular tasks you want the groups of your people to face. Any age group can play a version of RALPH. You might give each shelter group a particular theological stance on which they must base their decisions. This would be an excellent way to have your people experience the implications of certain ethical positions. Bounce around these probes from the folk at Baldwin Community Methodist Church. Do something with these ideas with your folk. Let a planning committee strike these mind-flints and discover their own sparks. It is amazingly easy to make your own design. The results your people will glean from this idea will stun you. Try it, brothers and sisters.

GAMBIT SIX: BLIND

Our goal was clear. The large suburban church wanted to set up an event by which some adults and young people could communicate authentically. They had tired it before. It had been a disaster. Two hundred people had attended the public meeting. A moderator spoke concerning youth. The adults and young people quickly polarized. A man at the back of the room stood with a red face waving his fist in the air. He attacked the young people for their lack of responsibility. He attacked them for the lack of cleanliness. He attacked them for their disrespect of their elders. The teenager on the other side of the room stood with slow burning anger. His fists were clenched at his side. He spoke out concerning the hypocrisy of adults. He attacked the affluency of that church. He ridiculed the self-righteousness of those in the room. A collision between unmovable people.

The committee of adults and young people wanted to go beyond this particular encounter. We wanted something that would enable people to relate to each other as persons. Ten adults and young people met five times in the next few weeks. We planned an all day event built around a simulation game we labeled BLIND. It was our task to enable people to simulate the experience of having to probe as persons on a level that would give them sight through different kinds of eyes.

The first time we were together was very important. It was a process of decompressing their past expectations and experiences. Most planning groups have to shake off somehow the limitations that had been placed on them by limiting learning experiences. They admitted that they had never played, let alone designed, a simulation game. The planning adults and young people did have a good basis of personal communication. They trusted each other. They had had a fine weekend experience of role playing. Things began to happen. Ideas began to bounce around the room. Pretty soon people lost track of who had originated an idea. The ideas suddenly became everybody's possession.

GAMING

At the end of the meeting a pattern began to emerge. We realized we had to put forth ideas that would open up people's minds and experiences but at the same time protect their dignity and their sensitivities.

Task groups went out in several directions of research and study before the next meeting. As the design of the event began to emerge, it was clear that we wanted to build the full day's experience into a basic liturgical form. We grasped onto the passage in 1 John 2:7-11. The contrast between light and darkness seemed to have all kinds of meanings. The church was large enough that we could count on the fact that most of the members did not know one another.

Eighty people appeared on the day of the event. They had been told to wear casual clothing. When the game began they were effectively blindfolded. The task groups had carefully worked out the design of the simulation game. Five different environments had been designed. These obstacle settings were simply religious education rooms.

Room 1 was a classroom totally emptied of furniture. On the floor, the task force in charge of this room had designed a maze with masking tape. The maze was a very complicated, twisting path that led through the room and out the other door. The group of eighty people was divided into sub-groups or teams of ten or twelve people. Each team had to go through Room 1 on hands and knees because of the blindfolds. Their hands were the guides that enabled them to get through the room. If one person got lost, all members of the team were restarted at the beginning.

Room 2 was filled with empty cardboard boxes. Each team was told to build a place of protection using the empty boxes. What the groups were not told was that someone had been planted in the room to keep pulling down what had been built up. This was designed to force them to work as a team to overcome this handicap. One team immediately realized what was happening. It formed a human chain around the building area for protection. One member then did the building.

Room 3 (actually two rooms) provided an experience where part of the group heard only the sound track and part of the group saw only the visual portion of a film. This was done by taking one sub-group into a room where they heard the sound which had been pre-recorded on a tape cassette. Members of the other group, in an adjoining room, removed their blindfolds temporarily to watch the film without the sound track. The sections of the teams were then re-united, and they talked about what some had seen and others had heard. The film chosen had a sound track which related to the visual only on an emotional level. We were hoping that they would communicate on the feeling level of their experience.

Room 4 was an environment where a woman was present as a mystery person. The teams were urged to design a way they could find out the character and personal qualities of this person with only limited data. They could ask six questions of her and touch her feet, hands, and face. We were trying to enable them to become very sensitive to subtle ways by which people communicate personality.

Room 5 offered an opportunity for members

22

of all the teams to probe each other. We had asked them during the opening liturgical preparation to make an offering to God by putting some object from their person which best reflected who they were into a plastic bag with a string on it. This bag was then put around each person's neck by means of the string. In room 5 each person took his object and passed it around the group. Each person then made comments on what he thought the object felt like and what it said about the person who chose it.

After each group had completed a thirty-minute stay in each environment, the whole group was led back to the large room used at the beginning. The liturgical structure was resumed. The groups were then separated, their members were placed in different parts of the room. The scriptural passage was read again and blindfolds ritualistically removed. The gathered students were then asked to find the people they had been with for the past two and a half hours. It was amazing how soon everyone had found his group. They then continued their worship by going to a love feast (spaghetti dinner). The associate minister at the church introduced the confession of sins aspect of the worship by walking behind each person with a mirror. He would hold the mirror before a person and ask him to confess before God and his brothers and sisters something about which he feels ashamed, as it was reflected in the image before him. The bearer of the mirror then gave a personal word of assurance for the forgiveness of sins.

After the dinner, people suggested that they would like to get back into their groups and talk about the experience they had had together and other things on their minds.

When we had our staff debriefing we experienced mixed feelings. We rejoiced over the depth and warmth of the experience among the participants. There was clear indication that some new kinds of relationships had been established. However, we were also frustrated in our initial concern for a meeting of minds on certain issues which had divided people previously. This experience made us realize how goals should be sharply defined at the beginning so there will not be unnecessary disappointment at the conclusion. We also had failed to build this event into a long-range strategy. We were caught in the kind of danger faced by most church experiences. Special learning events are usually isolated happenings which do not complement a rhythm of learning and growing. There is a real temptation to try each new fad method of teaching as an isolated "special" and thereby not suck all the nourishment out of it. Creative teaching approaches only have validity when anchored firmly to local goals and needs.

BLIND is certainly not the perfect or most fitting game for everyone. However, we are continually suggesting that you take these probes and adjust them to your needs and your people. It just may happen that one facet of the total game may trigger an idea for something that you can create for and with your people. Be free. Do your own playing and learning!

GAMING

Let's recap the structure of BLIND.

GOAL: To enable a group of people to play at discovering nonvisual ways of seeing and knowing others.

TOOLS:
1. A planning group of 4-8 people. Scripture focus 1 John 2:7-11.
2. A group of adults and young people.
3. Several empty classrooms.
4. Blindfolds.
5. Plastic bags with strings on them.
6. Short experimental film with collagelike sound and visual style.
7. Cassette for taping sound track.
8. Masking tape.
9. Cardboard boxes.
10. Facilities and arrangements organized for dinner (love feast).
11. Mirror.

STEPS:
1. Planning group brainstorms the design for the event.
2. A careful reading of 1 John 2:7-11.
3. Task group preparation of the rooms to be used.
4. A suggested design for the maze room:

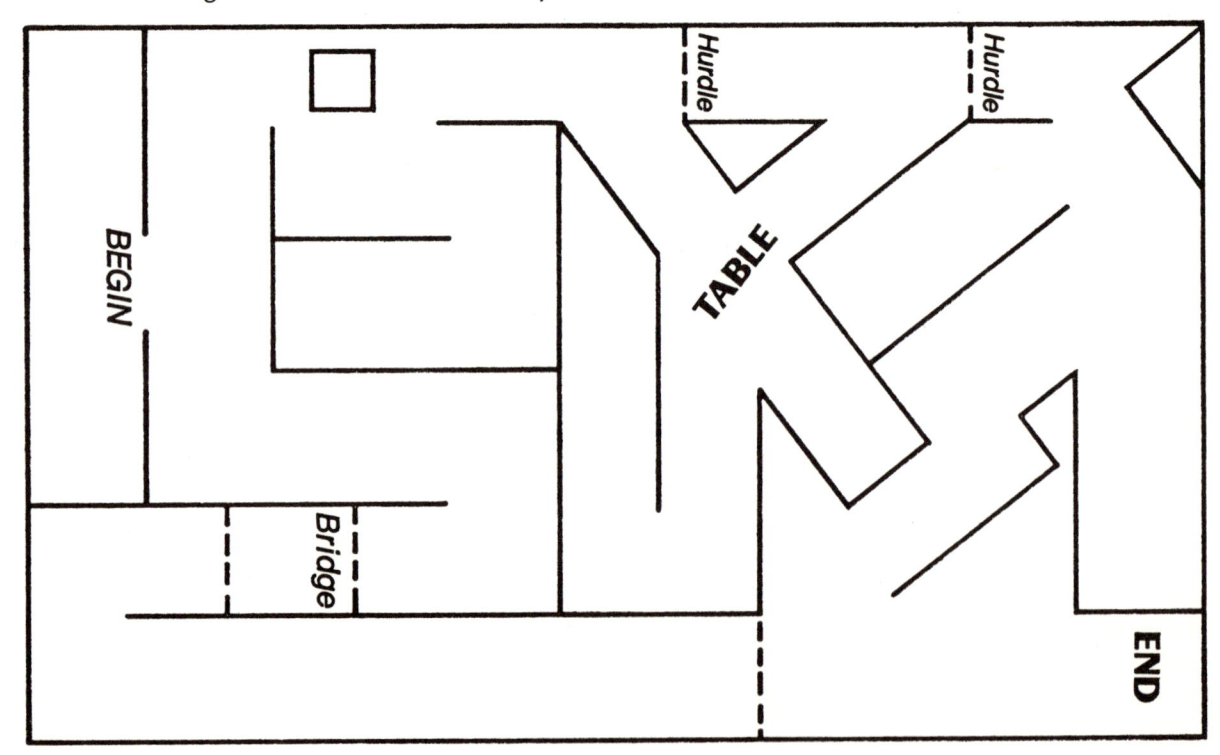

24

5. A suggested recorded (or orally read) message of instructions for the maze room:

"Welcome to the world of the unknown. Forget the existence of the past. You have become blind mice in a maze. All your instructions will come from me and I am a tape recording. There is another human in this room. He cannot speak and takes all orders from me.

"You are now at the start of the maze. It has no walls and almost no physical barriers at all. The guidelines are strips of tape on the floor. You must not step outside the guidelines.

"The end of the maze is some distance away and can only be reached by cooperation, teamwork, and communication. A member of your group has been given an object. He now knows what it is but may not tell any other member. This object will be placed at the end of the maze and the only way you will know you have reached the end is if this person can again identify it.

"If any member of your team becomes hopelessly lost, stand up and the entire group will be returned to the beginning. The group will start over if anyone steps outside the boundaries."

GAMBIT SIX BLIND

OPTIONAL ENDINGS
  a. "You have reached the end. Do you have all of your members?"
  b. "You have several minutes before you must continue your journey. Perhaps you would like to use this time to discuss what has happened here."
6. Invitations and publicity are prepared with some indication of the experiential character of the event ("dress casually").
7. Finalize the liturgical structure of the whole event. One suggested is as follows:
   a. CALL TO WORSHIP (Items of concern selected from that day's newspaper.)
   b. TEXT IS READ (1 John 2:7-11)
   c. SYMBOLS OF OUR SALVATION (Paper, sunglasses, etc.)
   d. PEOPLE'S RESPONSE (Offering: Items are chosen by each participant from his person and put into a plastic bag. The objects are to be chosen as best representing that person. The bags are hung around each person's neck.)
   e. PRAYER OF THANKSGIVING (Each person responds to the question: If everything were to be taken away from you what one thing would you want to retain?)

GAMING

    f. SERMON (Enacted Word of God. People are blindfolded and proceed to act the passage from darkness to light—hatred to love.)
    g. RECEIVING THE LIGHT (People return to the main room to the sound of the Beatles' song, "Here Comes the Sun." People are mixed up and given sight again.)
    h. CONFESSION (Groups are now sitting at tables at the love feast. Mirror is passed around and each person confesses what he sees in the mirror about which he needs forgiveness.)
    i. ASSURANCE OF PARDON (The bearer of the mirror touches each person on the shoulders and gives assurance of forgiveness.)
    j. LOVE FEAST (Eating and celebrating.)
    k. INTERCESSION (Washing or wiping of feet [shoes] with blindfolds.)
    l. FELLOWSHIP (Debriefing in groups.)
    m. DEPARTING (Whispering one to the other, "I love you, Christ loves you!")

BLIND is a highly structured game. We experimented with the living liturgy format. Such a probe may or may not be the thing for your setting. You might just latch on to the idea of the obstacle rooms. Your folk might have a very different goal or objective in mind as you claim aspects of this idea for your own game. It is important that you realize that ideas don't belong to anyone.

I suspect that real creativity is just the miraculously simple act of reordering the existing fragments of human existence into new meaningful forms. This kind of broad barn-door definition of creativity includes everybody everywhere doing everything. However, so many of the brothers and sisters are timid about their commitments to their God that they will not see themselves as creative beings. Shame on them.

This kind of creativity is based on the locus of new creation as being the community. Theologically this is very easy for us to acknowledge. The community is the occasion of the Holy Spirit (Acts 2). If we accept these understandings of creativity, it means that a new fluidity must be manifested in our treatment of ideas and designs. What we have done in creating games belongs to you. There is no longer competition between us. This is not the old rivalry which exists in so many communities. Churches down the street from each other will not undertake a similar kind of education methodology or teaching style because someone else has done it first. In our kind of learning and creating I rejoice when I discover that you are also excited about something that turns me on. In my recognition of your creativity I am finding affirmation of my identity. This gives me the freedom to admit that some aspects of our games did not work as well as we had hoped. We expose our failures in order to save you the problems we have encountered.

BLIND can be used by you in many ways. The actual sections of 1 John 2:7-11 might be more closely related to each environment. Such a closely related biblical overlay would have enabled the participants to experience Scripture and realize more completely what they were doing. Our debriefing on this event was not as strong or as complete as that we experienced in the RALPH game. I guess that I had learned more by then.

Take BLIND and use its mind flints anyway that you can. Let the ideas or sparks flow through your spirit. Don't resist any idea or contact point between what we did and what you might do. Don't start out being sensible and worried about feasibility. There are always means by which an idea can be worked. The actual spark is the source of all else. Let BLIND work on you and your folk. Then plunge out in a meaningful direction for your own event. You can do it in the best way possible. Only you and your folk can design that which will really touch the lives of your people. Nobody. Nobody at a distance can do it better than you.

GAMBIT SEVEN:

BREAD

This simulation game grew out of a group of local people's probe for a meaningful summer program of study. The group actually designed four simulation games without any previous experience or knowledge of this style of learning. BREAD was one of the most amazing experiences. The subcommittee designed it in a matter of several days.

Ray and his folk decided to use balloons as a means of visualizing the material status of a number of mythical countries. Each pair of players represented a country and had the responsibility of feeding their people. The green balloons stood for the food situations. The red balloons represented people. The population kept increasing by one hundred thousand people (1 red balloon) every five minutes. If there was a shortage of food, the people balloon was broken by the World Controller. People could get more food by trading with their neighbors or going to the Common Market. This was the process of placing a food balloon on a dart board and having the World Controller throw a dart. If he missed, two additional food balloons were given to the country that risked in this way. A broken balloon meant total loss of that resource.

GOAL: To enable us to experience the dynamics involved in feeding a starving population.

TOOLS: 1. Several rooms, each room containing:
    a. Tables with chairs.
    b. Red and green balloons.
    c. Slips of paper with "crisis situations" on them.
    d. Dart board and dart.

STEPS: 1. Split up into sub-groups of odd numbers (7, 9, etc.).
2. Each sub-group enters a room containing tools.
3. Sub-groups choose one person to act as "Controller."

4. Controller pairs off remaining players. Assigns each pair the name of a country. Distributes equal number of red and green balloons to each "country."
5. Controller explains rules:
   a. Each green balloon stands for enough food to feed one hundred thousand people. Each red balloon stands for one hundred thousand people.
   b. At 5-minute intervals Controller will burst all "people" balloons which cannot be fed by "food" balloons.
   c. Players may beg, steal, or trade to get enough food.
   d. Players may risk food balloons on the "World Common Market" by attaching balloon to dart board. Controller throws dart. If he misses he returns the balloon plus two others. If he hits—one hundred thousand people face starvation.
   e. Periodically the Controller distributes slips of paper containing special "crisis situations." (For example: War—lose two red balloons, take one green balloon from another country. Population boom—take three red balloons from Controller. Crop failure—lose four green balloons, etc.).
6. When the game is beginning to roll along, after an hour or so, Controller stops it for debriefing. The sub-groups discuss their behavior. How does this apply to actual world problems? How does the morality they have applied contrast with the biblical injunction to have mercy?
7. Game is continued. After another period of play the sub-groups assemble and share insights.

This basically simple structure netted some unexpected results. People immediately pursued the profit motive. A few nations started collecting more and more wealth. Other nations were getting closer and closer to starvation. There was intense competition. People were playing the game seriously. Yet, no one suggested sharing the food wealth. Midway in the game the game masters announced that a special message had come from the World Federation of Church Bodies. The message was simply "for I was hungry and you gave me food . . . (Matt. 25:35 ff.). This did not even change the thrust of the competition. Red people balloons began to explode with hunger.

During the debriefing each group struggled with the problem of ethically dealing with hunger. To begin the evening, the people were to have a meal. Each person was served exactly what seventeen cents would buy. We had wanted the people to experience a bit of the hunger problem. One man said that he realized now that he played harder because he was a bit hungry and wanted to be sure that he had "food." They had a hard time working on the

GAMING

Christian ethic for a time of poverty. What emerged from this session for the leadership was an excellent picture of how the church has failed really to deal with the response of the affluent as they face suffering. Do you just give it all away? How do you keep your offerings for the poor from being tokenism? What do you do when you know that world economics destroys the weak and yet you can't do anything about it? How do you live with powerlessness? This game actually forced some long-range planning on the group.

We do not often look at learning experiences as revealing directions where we should go in other experiences. Perhaps BREAD will enable you to open up some interest areas for your people. Your own creative use of this game may give you directions for the future.

One teacher used a modified version of BREAD only to find that important side issues were raised by her ninth graders. She happened to choose red and black balloons. One boy was running out of food balloons (red). He simply broke the black (people) balloon himself. The teacher asked why he had done that instead of waiting for the Controller to do it. "Well, I figured that the balloon probably represented black people. I can do without them." This isolated experience in the game opened a frank discussion on racism for the whole class. The teacher pushed the other kids to see if they agreed. The others said they didn't. She then asked why they didn't object to what he was saying and had done in the game.

A game like this is so easy to design yourself with your people. Be free as you plan for something like this. Feel free to change the game and the rules in any way. You will be amazed to see how well your people can design a game with these kinds of factors involved. Try BREAD and slice it any way you desire.

GAMBIT EIGHT:
FLIGHT 108

A committee of four designed this event as one session in the series of meetings (Sunday school) on ethics. We were limited by having only an hour. There were adults and young people coming to this class. We wanted to open this series with something which would lay bare just what their functional ethical system really was.

We decided to play FLIGHT 108. This game grows out of a combination of ideas from movies and the book, *Situation Ethics* (Joseph Fletcher [Philadelphia: Westminster, 1966]). We liked the idea of people having to make decisions and then analyzing on what basis they had come to such conclusions.

Chris and Dave spent the week interviewing people with a cassette tape recorder. They asked each person why they felt that life was worth living. We carefully chose people from different age and occupational backgrounds. I edited the tapes into one unit. Dave also took a Polaroid picture of each person. We pasted these photos on an 8½" by 14" sheet of paper. An electronic stencil was then made for the mimeograph machine. We also obtained the use of an old opaque projector.

(*Note:* In some localities it may be difficult to find means for making an electronic stencil. If you encounter difficulty, perhaps the best solution would be to number the photographs and display them on an easel so that the students can all see them as they make their decisions.)

On the Sunday morning of the meeting we told the students that the sheet of paper that they held contained the twelve passengers who were on FLIGHT 108. They were people who loved life. The class was charged with the task of collecting data on them. The students were going to have to choose five people who were to live. This flight was going to crash. It was up to them to spare five people. They could make notes on their mimeographed sheets as we played the tape and projected large images of the pictures on the sheet with the opaque projector.

GAMING

The raps from the people were short, but powerful. A mother of four was pictured in her living room. She quietly stated that her life had not been very important. However, her family was the key to her life. "I want to live just to see that my children grow up to be good people." A black accountant in a downtown office spoke about how she hated the slum she was forced to live in. "I want to live in order to make a better life. My greatest dream is to get a decent apartment." The gas station owner was fifty-nine years old. He loved life because he had done a lot. He had traveled around the world. "If I had to die now, I would have no regret." The college student was taped at a young people's meeting. "I have given my life to Christ. I feel that he has called me to do something for the young people of Upper St. Clair. I want to live in order to fulfill this calling."

A young assistant minister spoke about his desire to meet the responsibilities of his family. "I want to live to be the kind of parent my children will need in order to be the kind of adults they must become." The janitor at the high school dreamed about retirement. His memories included a lot of happiness about the young people he had served. "I just want to get into retirement and live happily with my wife after so many years of work." The twenty-two-year-old ex-coffeehouse manager didn't have a job when he was interviewed. A long silence hung in the air before he answered the question about why he wanted to live. "I guess that I have no reason that is practical. I just dig life and people. I have no plans or dreams."

The secretary was just a year away from retirement. She admitted that life had been hard since her husband died. It was lonely. There had been a long hard fight to put her sons through college. "I still want to live. I want to see my children and grandchildren live full lives." The young secretary at the desk next to her looked to her forthcoming marriage as her main reason for living. "I just want to love my husband fully and any future children we might have." John was about to complete his high school work. He wanted to live in order to change the corrupt society. "The social system is destroying both the rich and the poor. Socialism is the only answer for our country and the world." At the bottom of the sheet were two small children. One was two and the other was four. They just stood there with smiles on their faces. There was no rap from them.

After exposing them to this visual and sound experience we divided the class into three subgroups. Each group had to agree on the person they chose. Just before the sub-groups were to rejoin the whole class, I told them that there had been a change. "You are on the plane and six people are to live. Who will that extra person be?"

Recap of FLIGHT 108

GOAL: To enable the students to realize what their ethical premises were for making decisions.

TOOLS: 1. An enabling group.
2. Tape interviews and Polaroid pictures of 12-20 people.
3. Mimeograph set or easel display of pictures of the passenger lists.

GAMBIT EIGHT   FLIGHT 108

            4. As much time as you can get.

STEPS: 1. Preparation by enabling group.
2. Give out paper and play tape (and show pictures if possible).
3. Divide major group into smaller work groups.
4. Set them to the task of deciding which five persons will live from the list.
5. Change task to include them on the plane and six will live.
6. Bring the group together and discuss the basis of their decisions.
7. Record results on a blackboard.
8. Have them try to cope with the reasons behind their ethical decisions.

When the group came back together the responses were very interesting. Just about every possible ethical position had been taken. Some let "fate" decide. Others based their decision on "usefulness." Others based such decisions on how "faithful" people had seemed.

The thrust of the course was established by this game. We did not resolve the problem. However, I was able then to follow the major ethical systems they had used in following sessions.

Remember that such a suggestive model of a game can be changed in many ways. Be free to explore how you can develop your own design for your people. The whole gaming thing is just a style of giving parabolic form to the essence you are trying to explore.

Such use of teaching forms is based on several premises. In the first place, we are moving from a base of experiential education. This is the concept which hunches that content, particularly theology, can best be integrated with the full experience of understanding and life by doing what is being said. Form and content then become inseparable.

Secondly, we are also working from the assumption that the process of teaching should stem from the student's baggage. What the student brings to the learning experience in terms of past life events is part of what must be learned. This means that such teaching puts a lot of confidence in the students. There is a basic respect and concern for the one who learns.

The third premise behind such educational probes is that local enablers can do creative things when working in community. The best way teachers discover their potential is when they develop their own materials in community. Your people will amaze you if they try to design or adapt some of these kinds of gaming possibilities. The next time you try to do something they will urge a new style of teaching. A creative learning experience tends to breed more creativity if nurtured.

The fourth foundation for my kind of teaching is that I love the people I am called to serve. I assume that they will respond to authentic teaching probes. This means that I am not uptight about a person who might resist playing FLIGHT 108 or some other design. I will try to incorporate this hostility into the game in order to further the study process of the players.

This kind of game can open up all kinds of student concerns. The question of age against

GAMING

youth in terms of value to the society may jump out at those playing. The whole question of human "worth" as one of the standards of survival will quickly be forwarded by some.

FLIGHT 108 should spin some gaming ideas within your planning group. Don't worry about the changes you will have to make. Be free to experiment in terms of your people and the goals you have chosen. You might recycle this idea by having people within the group be the passengers. The major group then has a chance to have each person speak about why he wants to be saved. There can be a press conference game set up. This could be a fantastic way of having people relive the kinds of decisions that they make each day. After the decisions have been made, have the passengers react to the decisions. Maybe the flight mates can play their own game or decide who will stay and who will go. This is what they could do while the others are making their decisions. You will be pleasantly surprised by the quality of the game you can create from his mind flint. The response of your people will break open channels of ethical discussion perhaps never before part of your religious education experience. Try it!

GAMBIT NINE:
FIG LEAF AND EAST OF EDEN

This crazy game first bloomed as a committee of young people and adults shared audio cassette tapes back and forth with me concerning a forthcoming event. They were in the state of Washington and I was in Pittsburgh. As we let our minds bounce back and forth, a new design took shape.

One of the basic purposes of the conference was to enable the 250 young people and adults from the Pacific Northwest to be a community of love and faith as they faced the problems of today.

The conference met in a fantastic setting of ocean, sand, and trees. I gathered the whole body of people. I read Genesis 1 and told them that I was going to divide them into tribes. Each tribe had all day to get itself together and rebuild a whole new world, as if it were back in Eden. They could change everything. However, the group could not use English. Each tribe had to bring back a message to be shared with the other tribes.

Well, the campers were stunned. They didn't know how to communicate. Finally a few people started to invent a new language. One tribe just ran off to get it together through physical activity (bouncing a ball to each other on the beach). They left behind an older person. I asked another tribe what its responsibility was to this person. They immediately took her into their tribe. They invented an adoption rite on the spot. Each person bowed down before her and then stood up and hugged her.

A number of the leadership adults were uptight about the event. Where were the leaders to direct the young people in their problem solving task? One woman tried to get her young people to revolt against the design. The adults who had planned this event with me spent a great deal of time with this woman's reaction to our game. Some very important side ministry developed with her as a result of her contribution of anger. Always remain sensitive to the secondary or side games that may be played as spin-offs of your major game. People must play out their reactions to situations as best

35

GAMING

they can. It is up to the leadership to use these energies in a constructive manner.

The results of that evening at the gathering of the tribes were unbelievable. Some groups had made items to express a message of love to the others. For instance, one tribe had taken vines along the beach and made a long rope. This rope was woven through the gathering of people while the tribe hummed, "They Know that We Are Christians by Our Love." Another group passed out pieces of seashells which had been crudely hammered into crosses. They motioned with their hands for this small symbol to be passed along to your neighbor.

Other tribes used pictures to express their basic messages. Each person in one tribe had a symbol and a name in their own language. Another group used a ball to express solidarity among the persons at the general gathering. They passed the ball around the circle. One tribe embraced each person present. Love and peace were themes central to each tribe's message. They were struggling with the problem of presenting their faith in the most basic way possible. The participants were quite thrilled that they could express such love and that it was understandable without words.

One teacher friend has adapted this basic game to a design that she had her junior high young people play in an hour. They quickly grasped the possibilities of building a new society. Many of the young people were worried about man's destruction of what God had given. During the debriefing members of the class criticized one girl who spent her whole time cleaning herself by their imaginary stream. They felt that she was making the water unfit to drink. What does one do with the gift fresh from God's hands?

Recap of FIG LEAF

GOAL: To enable the students to experience the process of communicating on the most basic level—and make primitive probes of relating to other close groups of people.

TOOLS: 1. Enabling groups of planners.
2. A careful reading of Genesis 1–3.
3. A group of adult and young people ranging in size from 50 to 300.
4. Lots of space.
5. A full weekend of time, or for shorter versions an hour.

STEPS: 1. Call assembly of people together and tell them the task: to rebuild a new world in the context of Genesis 1.
2. Divide into tribes (mixing up kids from different groups).
3. Instruct them to do their task without using existing languages. Tell them to bring back a message that can be communicated to the other tribes when you gather again in four or five hours.
4. Have the groups share messages (one tribe at a time) when they gather.
5. This meeting can be celebration or worship.

A companion aspect of this game was a second part called EAST OF EDEN. This name comes from Genesis 3. The second day they met again as tribes and were asked to continue their reconstruction of the fallen environment and use English. They got very uptight. After the nonverbal intensity of the previous day, the many words about the problems outside of Eden seemed phony.

In another setting, the second part of the game was enacted by sending the participants into the world (commune, bus station, airport, shopping center). They were told to interview people and find out who they are. Then the tribe must make a media presentation of the hope they could offer to the needs found in the particular persons they encountered in the world. One tribe came back with the exciting

GAMBIT NINE FIG LEAF (AND EAST OF EDEN)

report that they had found a woman who had suffered a recent death in her family and was waiting alone in the airport. She thanked them for caring about her.

You can play this game in many different ways. It is really the experiential teaching of Scripture. Why not play with the Scriptures? Maybe this can be the most valid means of getting into Scripture. I have suggested more particular avenues for this kind of Scripture study in the SOS (Switched On Scripture) enabling cassette tapes for the Abingdon audio•graphics materials.

The New and Old Testaments suggest many gaming possibilities. Once you and your enabling group catch this play bug, ideas will give you many game structures. Start this process with FIG LEAF and EAST OF EDEN.

GAMBIT TEN: CRUNCH

This game grew out of the study series at Southminster United Presbyterian Church. The committee of young people and adults really went wild once they concocted the design. We decided to have the students confront the problem of war through a game of their creation.

The enabling group constructed a map of a mythical cluster of nations. They dotted their imaginary landscape with names derived from church personnel. The task group developed a careful set of plans concerning a world crisis. Each player was paired with another person. These working partners were cast as representatives of the countries involved in this international situation. They were told that they were participants in an international conference called to solve the escalating crisis. Each team was presented with a folder containing the position taken by their government. They had to bargain from this position in their country's interest.

The game master was introduced as the Moderator from the International Council of Churches for this bargaining meeting. He told the participants that the unfortunate assassination of one nation's leader and the following armed conflict between nations had to be resolved. As the game proceeded the players found that they were locked into positions of self-interest by the given instructions. There were several breaks for caucusing between nations. The crunch of the nations caught in this conflict was acutely experienced by the players.

The game was stopped after the tension had grown. The Moderator then set before the groups a number of biblical positions about peace and love. "What bearing does Christ's commandment to turn the other cheek have to do with what has happened here?" "Do you think that a nation can lay down its life for its neighbor?" The lingering difficulties of contemporary history seemed to feed into this theological probe. Here are the documents presented to the participants:

FROM: World Council of Churches For Peace

CHRISTIAN BROTHERS:

    We entreat you to remember Christ's message of peace and brotherhood as members of His body on earth. Remember this message as you go to encounter this weighty problem, and endeavor to make your solution one which will be an example of His love to the world.

MAP of the CRISIS AREA

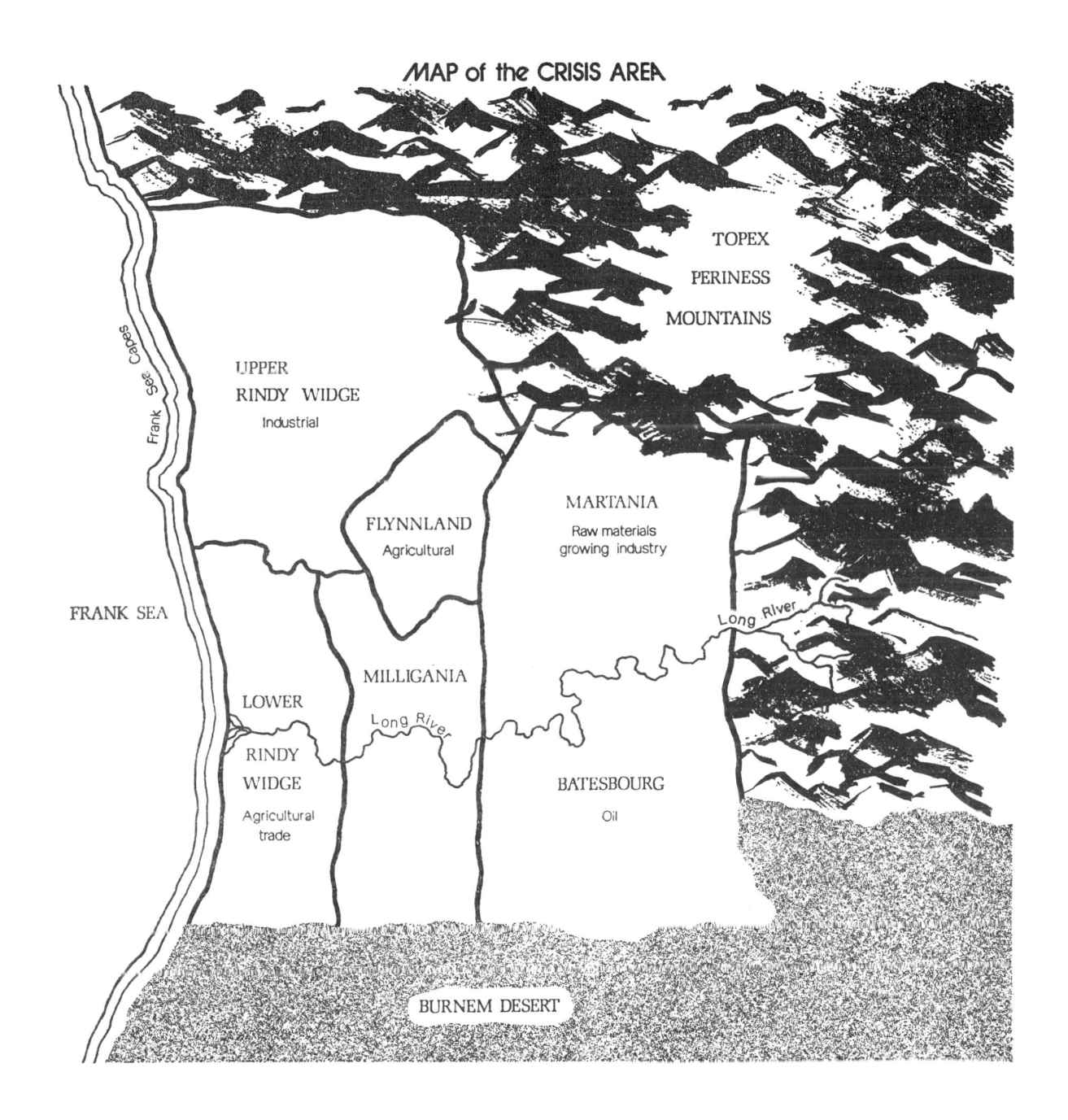

TOPEX PERINESS MOUNTAINS

UPPER RINDY WIDGE
Industrial

FLYNNLAND
Agricultural

MARTANIA
Raw materials
growing industry

Frank See Capes

FRANK SEA

Long River

MILLIGANIA
Long River

LOWER RINDY WIDGE
Agricultural
trade

BATESBOURG
Oil

BURNEM DESERT

Official Communique
Prime Minister
Republic of Batesbourg

THE SITUATION:

Upper Rindy Widge has a complex industrial society based on Lower Rindy Widge's agriculture and raw materials from our northern neighbors, Martania. As you know, Martania has, with our aid, begun to develop its own economy. With growing stability, the people of Martania have started to resent our influence, claiming we are stifling their freedom.

Meanwhile, our neighbors, Upper Rindy Widge, are experiencing grave economic recession due to the lack of Martania's raw materials, which they are now using themselves. This recession has caused their need for our oil to drop. This has had adverse effects on our economy.

Upper Rindy Widge recently sent a team of negotiators to Martania to discuss a mutual trade agreement. Because the Long and Narrow Pass was snowed over, the ambassadors traveled through Flynnland. This was during a festival celebrating their independence from Upper Rindy Widge. A group of Martanian radicals assassinated the ambassador.

Upper Rindy Widge has declared war on Martania to try to take back by force what has been denied them. Their route of attack is through neutral Flynnland. Most of their land will probably be destroyed—they have no other economy.

YOUR MISSION: TRY FOR A PEACEFUL SETTLEMENT THAT WILL PROTECT OUR INTERESTS. IF WAR IS THE ONLY ALTERNATIVE, ALLY WITH UPPER RINDY WIDGE. WE HAVE THE NEW WEAPON! DO NOT LET THIS BE KNOWN UNLESS YOU HAVE TO.

Official Government Communique
Office of the President
Republic of Milligania

THE SITUATION:

Upper Rindy Widge has a complex industrial society based entirely upon the agriculture of Lower Rindy Widge and the raw materials of Martania. Martania has begun to develop its own industrial society with capital from Batesbourg. (Batesbourg has a very primitive society, but the part of the Burnem Desert which extends into it is rich in oil, making a small percent-5%-very rich). However, with growing stability, the people of Martania have begun to resent Batesbourg's influence, which they feel is stifling their freedom.

Meanwhile, Upper Rindy Widge's economy is falling drastically because of the lack of Martania's raw materials which Martania is now using for itself.

U.R.W. recently sent ambassadors to Martania to make a mutual trade agreement. Because the one small mountain pass (Long and Narrow) between the U.R.W., Martania, and Flynnland was snowed over, the ambassadors traveled through Flynnland.

During a festival celebrating Flynnland's newly won independence from U.R.W., a group of Martanian radicals assassinated the ambassadors. This was a perfect excuse for U.R.W. to attack Martania and take the raw materials.

Upper Rindy Widge plans to invade Martania by marching across Flynnland. This wanton devastation of its rich land must be prevented at all costs, for they have no other economy.

Milligania depends on Batesbourg for its oil. Batesbourg threatens alliance with U.R.W. Most of our people have migrated from Flynnland. Thus we still have strong family ties. We control both Martania's and Batesbourg's access to the Frank Sea, on which both countries are dependent for marketing their products. But we are in turn dependent on Lower Rindy Widge for our only access to the Frank Sea, the Long River.

YOUR MISSION: TO PROTECT THE RIGHTS OF MARTANIA AND FLYNNLAND. BE SURE TO RETAIN OUR RIGHTS IN THE LONG RIVER. IF WAR IS THE ONLY ALTERNATIVE, ALLY WITH MARTANIA AND FLYNNLAND. WE HAVE A NEW WEAPON WHICH CAN QUICKLY DISABILITATE U.R.W. BEFORE IT CAN DESTROY FLYNNLAND. DO NOT LET THIS BE KNOWN UNLESS YOU HAVE TO!!!!!!

LOWER [LR/W] RINDY WIDGE

Official Communique
Office of the President
Republic of Lower Rindy Widge

THE SITUATION:

Our old ally Upper Rindy Widge has a complex industrial society based entirely upon the agriculture of Lower Rindy Widge and the raw materials of Martania. Martania has begun to develop its own industrial society with capital from Batesbourg. (Batesbourg has a very primitive society, but the part of the Burnem Desert which extends into it is rich in oil, making a small percentage of the people-5%- very rich). However, with growing stability, the people of Martania have begun to resent Batesbourg's influence, which they feel is stifling their freedom.

Meanwhile, Upper Rindy Widge's economy is failing drastically because of the lack of Martania's raw materials which Martania is now using for itself.

U.R.W. recently sent ambassadors to Martania to make a mutual trade agreement. Because the one small mountain pass (Long and Narrow) on the border between U.R.W. and Martania was snowed over, their ambassadors traveled through Flynnland.

During a festival celebrating Flynnland's newly won independence from U.R.W., a group of Martanian radicals assassinated the ambassadors.

With their once-prosperous country now threatening deep depression, their children hungry, their men out of work, their shops and businesses closed down, this was the last straw. With the remaining resources, U.R.W. declared war on Martania. Their object is to gain back what Martania will not give them. They have no resources of their own. They are dependent on Martania's resources for over half their economy. Their economy is built on the prosperity brought from these resources, and they are lost without them.

Upper Rindy Widge, separated from us in the old colonial days, once again needs our support. We can help them since we control Milligania's, Batesbourg's, and Martania's access to the sea by way of the Long River.

We have word that Batesbourg may also help us.

Upper Rindy Widge's route of attack is through Flynnland. Although this may destroy some of their fields, it is totally necessary since they must reestablish their economy.

YOUR MISSION: TO HELP U.R.W. SAVE ITS ECONOMY,
THUS MAINTAINING OUR ECONOMY
BASED ON TRADE ESPECIALLY WITH
UPPER RINDY WIDGE.

URW

Official Communique
President of
The Republic of Upper Rindy Widge

THE SITUATION:

We have a complex industrial society based entirely upon the agriculture of Lower Rindy Widge and the raw materials of Martania. Martania has begun to develop its own industrial society with capital from Batesbourg. (Batesbourg has a very primitive society, but the part of the Burnem Desert which extends into it is rich in oil, making a small percentage of the people—5%—very rich). However, with growing stability, the people of Martania have begun to resent Batesbourg's influence, which they feel is stifling their freedom.

Meanwhile, our economy is failing drastically because of the lack of Martania's raw materials which Martania is now using for itself.

We recently sent ambassadors to Martania to make a mutual trade agreement. Because the one small mountain pass (Long and Narrow) on the border between U.R.W. and Martania was snowed over, our ambassadors traveled through Flynnland.

During a festival celebrating Flynnland's newly won independence from us, a group of Martanian radicals assassinated our ambassadors.

With our once-prosperous country now threatening deep depression, our children hungry, our men out of work, our shops and businesses closed down, this was the last straw. With our remaining resources, we have declared war on Martania. Our object is to gain back what Martania will not give us. We have no resources of our own. We are dependent on Martania's resources for over half our economy. Our economy is built on the prosperity brought from these resources, and we are lost without them.

Our old ally Lower Rindy Widge, separated from us in the old colonial days, has once again promised its support. This is good, since it controls Milligania's, Batesbourg's, and Martania's access to the sea by way of the Long River.

We have word that Batesbourg may also help us.

Our route of attack is through Flynnland. Although this may destroy some of their fields, it is totally necessary since we must reestablish our economy.

YOUR MISSION: SAVE OUR ECONOMY, OUR COUNTRY!!!!!!!

Office of the Prime Minister
PEOPLES REPUBLIC OF MARTANIA
Official Communique

THE SITUATION:

Until about ten years ago, Upper Rindy Widge based its highly complex industrial society upon our raw materials and the agriculture of Lower Rindy Widge. However, Batesbourg saw many possibilities in backing industry within our own country. (Batesbourg has a very primitive society, but the part of the Burnem dessert which extends into it is rich in oil, making a small percentage-5%- of the people, very rich.) Thus, we have had to cut our deliveries to U.R.W. in order to meet our own demands. As a result, U.R.W. claims that its economy will be in bankruptcy within the month. We know this is a highly exaggerated report since much of its economy is based not on our raw minerals but on processing L.R.W.'s food, cotton, etc.

Upper Rindy Widge sent ambassadors here to make a trade agreement last month. They were forced to take a route through Flynnland because the high mountain pass on our small border with U.R.W. was snowed in. During a festival celebrating Flynnland's newly won independence from U.R.W. a group of Martanian radicals (denounced by our country) assassinated the ambassadors. U.R.W. jumped at this excuse and declared war on us.

Upper Rindy Widge plans to invade Martania through Flynnland. It is to be expected that much of Flynnland's rich land will be devastated. Flynnland has no other economy.

Added to this, Batesbourg has been stifling our freedom. They attach more and more strings to the capital they once gave freely. They use their influence more and more. Their censorship of our media grows daily. Now, because they feel we have insulted them and they are overly roused by some militant uprisings in our country, they threaten to ally with U.R.W.

L.R.W. was once a part of U.R.W., but they were separated during the colonial days. Because of this and because L.R.W. depends on trade with U.R.W., L.R.W. can be expected to ally with U.R.W.

This may be detrimental, but we know that we can count on Flynnland and probably Milligania for help. This is good because Milligania controls Batesbourg's access to the Frank Sea (via the Long River) and the block formed by Milligania, Flynnland, and us will also help to cut Batesbourg off from U.R.W. and L.R.W.

YOUR MISSION: TO PROTECT OUR INDUSTRY, TO PROTECT FLYNNLAND, MEANWHILE TO MAINTAIN AS GOOD RELATIONS WITH L.R.W. AS POSSIBLE IN ORDER TO INSURE AN OUTLET FOR OUR PRODUCTS. WE SUSPECT THAT EITHER MILLIGANIA OR BATESBOURG HAS A SECRET WEAPON BUT WE DON'T KNOW WHICH. DO NOT REVEAL THIS INFORMATION UNLESS YOU FEEL IT IS NECESSARY.

Peoples Republic of FLYNNLAND
Office of the Prime Minister

Official Communique

THE SITUATION:

Upper Rindy Widge has a complex industrial society based entirely upon the agriculture of Lower Rindy Widge and the raw materials of Martania. Martania has begun to develop its own industrial society with capital from Batesbourg. (Batesbourg has a very primitive society, but the part of the Burnem Desert which extends into it is rich in oil, making a small percent-5%-very rich.) However, with growing stability, the people of Martania have begun to resent Batesbourg's influence, which they feel is stifling their freedom.

Meanwhile, Upper Rindy Widge's economy is failing drastically because of the lack of Martania's raw materials which Martania is now using for itself.

Upper Rindy Widge recently sent ambassadors to Martania to make a mutual trade agreement. Because the one small mountain pass (Long and Narrow) between Upper Rindy Widge, Martania, and Flynnland was snowed over, the ambassadors traveled through Flynnland.

During a festival celebrating our newly won independence from U.R.W., a group of Martanian radicals assassinated the ambassadors. This was a perfect excuse for U.R.W. to attack Martania and take the raw materials. Now U.R.W. plans to invade Martania by marching across our land. This wanton devastation of our land must be prevented at all costs, for we have no other economy.

We hope that Milligania will support us, since most of their people are our people, having migrated from Flynnland within the last centuries. This will provide a fairly substantial block between U.R.W. and Batesbourg, should Batesbourg carry out its threat to join U.R.W. However, try to maintain peace (and protect our land) at all costs.

YOUR MISSION: TO MAINTAIN PEACE. BUT IF PEACE LOOKS
                       IMPROBABLE, TRY TO ALLY WITH MILLIGANIA
                       AND MARTANIA. WE HAVE INSIDE INFORMATION
                       THAT MARTANIA HAS DEFINITE PROMISE OF
                       SUPPORT IN ANY EVENT FROM A MAJOR OUTSIDE
                       POWER, AND MILLIGANIA HAS DEVELOPED A
                       SECRET WEAPON CAPABLE OF DESTROYING U.R.W.
                       BEFORE IT CAN DESTROY US.

Peoples Republic of FLYNNLAND
Office of the Prime Minister

Official Communique

THE SITUATION:

Upper Rindy Widge has a complex industrial society based entirely upon the agriculture of Lower Rindy Widge and the raw materials of Martania. Martania has begun to develop its own industrial society with capital from Batesbourg. (Batesbourg has a very primitive society, but the part of the Burnem Desert which extends into it is rich in oil, making a small percent-5%-very rich.) However, with growing stability, the people of Martania have begun to resent Batesbourg's influence, which they feel is stifling their freedom.

Meanwhile, Upper Rindy Widge's economy is failing drastically because of the lack of Martania's raw materials which Martania is now using for itself.

Upper Rindy Widge recently sent ambassadors to Martania to make a mutual trade agreement. Because the one small mountain pass (Long and Narrow) between Upper Rindy Widge, Martania, and Flynnland was snowed over, the ambassadors traveled through Flynnland.

During a festival celebrating our newly won independence from U.R.W., a group of Martanian radicals assassinated the ambassadors. This was a perfect excuse for U.R.W. to attack Martania and take the raw materials. Now U.R.W. plans to invade Martania by marching across our land. This wanton devastation of our land must be prevented at all costs, for we have no other economy.

We hope that Milligania will support us, since most of their people are our people, having migrated from Flynnland within the last centuries. This will provide a fairly substantial block between U.R.W. and Batesbourg, should Batesbourg carry out its threat to join U.R.W. However, try to maintain peace (and protect our land) at all costs.

YOUR MISSION: TO MAINTAIN PEACE. BUT IF PEACE LOOKS
                         IMPROBABLE, TRY TO ALLY WITH MILLIGANIA
                         AND MARTANIA. WE HAVE INSIDE INFORMATION
                         THAT MARTANIA HAS DEFINITE PROMISE OF
                         SUPPORT IN ANY EVENT FROM A MAJOR OUTSIDE
                         POWER, AND MILLIGANIA HAS DEVELOPED A
                         SECRET WEAPON CAPABLE OF DESTROYING U.R.W.
                         BEFORE IT CAN DESTROY US.

Recap of CRUNCH

GOAL: To enable a group of people to experience the crunch of hostility between nations and peoples when self-interest comes first.

TOOLS:
1. Maps of area of conflict.
2. Position papers for each delegation.
3. Moderator who gives information and keeps the lines of understanding open between players.
4. Selected biblical materials concerning the crunch of conflict and peace.
5. Place cards with the names of the countries.

STEPS:
1. Divide group into rooms of paired people who are told that they represent a particular country.
2. As they walk into room they find their places, each person is then given instructions from his government.
3. The Moderator sets the stage by retracing what has happened in the conflict.
4. The bargaining then starts.
5. After forty or so minutes of play, the biblical material is introduced for discussion.
6. Debriefing takes place.

Several of the people playing the game did not want to accept the positions of their government. They personally wanted to make peace, but did not have that directive from their nation. Two of the men in one delegation secretly pledged peace and plotted to overthrow their government on return to their country. They would do this by any means! One delegate felt that his nation had been insulted and stalked from the room at one point in a heated debate.

The country that had a secret weapon never mentioned it in the talks. The delegates seemed to be trying to keep this monster out of the picture. The players attempted statesmanship. However, they found that they were hindered by their official positions at every turn.

This basic design can be made much less complicated. There will be real excitement if you enable your people to design their own version of CRUNCH. You will be amazed how quickly they can develop a real situation for the conflict. Adults respond particularly well to this kind of game. Spin off your own game built around this mind flint.

GAMBIT ELEVEN:
MIND FLINTS

ACID is a simple little game which was developed to meet the needs of a Sunday morning class studying ethical systems. The adults and young people from the protected suburbs were tempted to stand off and fire criticism at other people who had to make ethical decisions. The planning team decided to design a game which would have the group playing without realizing that it was a game they were participating in.

A friend of mine took the role of a radical "hippy." I told the class that I would not be able to attend the next study session. I had to speak at a college in another city. I said that a person was invited who had a different value system than we did. They were supposed to find out why he did the things that he did.

Alan arrived wearing the whole denim uniform. He hardly spoke to anyone. He went to the coke dispenser and picked up an empty bottle. He turned on them with the bottle in his hand and waved it menacingly at the students. He kicked over a small table. He handed the bottle to a nearby man and asked him what he thought of when he felt the bottle. The man was very hostile back at Alan. Alan pressed everyone to make some comment about the bottle. He then talked about how the bottle could be made into a bomb to blow up the white establishment. He argued with the people about the evils of society.

About halfway through the session Alan started to change his presentation. He began using terminology that the churchmen would understand. He talked more and more about love. After about fifteen minutes of this, the people started to respond differently. One man volunteered that he did not personally accept all the things that Alan did, but he appreciated the reasons why he was concerned. Other people indicated that a bit of trust was developing. Alan played his hand fully by asking if they really trusted him. There were some nods of assent. He then reached into his pocket and produced a package of metal foil. He carefully unwrapped the silvery bundle. Alan acted as if he were trying not to touch the small dyed sugar cubes. He then systematically offered each person one of the strangely colored items. Alan assured each person that this was something that was really good for them. Each person refused the offer. Alan had trapped them into playing out their lack of real trust. They then explored this feeling and the ethical system on which he was acting.

This game is obviously an extension of old-fashioned role playing. In this case the whole group was pulled into a game without realizing what was happening.

THE MAGIC PILL is another spinoff of the ACID game. This game was designed for use in a course on drug abuse. It borrowed its technique heavily from basic role playing. The participants were given situations and roles to play. However, at key point in the playing each person would be given a candy pill. One color pill would be an "upper" and the other color would be a "downer." They were then supposed to alter their reactions accordingly. This gave the participants a chance to pass through a range of varying reactions to particular situations. The role of drugs and human problems was then probed.

KENT STATE is a game we designed in the course of a series of meetings. This game finds its structural source in matched role playing. Each person present was given a new identity and role. The situation is set in the town of Kent, Ohio, as things started to build up over student demands. The thirty people were divided into three different groups: students, administration, and town people. Each person within these groups was given a slip of paper which provided a new name and a paragraph on the position he or she takes in this situation. After having a groups caucus, there was a general meeting where the immediate problems were to be dealt with. This was an explosive meeting. There was lots of ironic humor in the confrontation. A conservative fifty-year-old man playing the role of a radical student wouldn't be seated during the meeting. He continually interrupted the meeting to make his radical points.

This then moved into an immediate debriefing. The teenagers and adults started speaking about the problems in their own church and the failure of people to listen to each other. KENT STATE was a timely game which enabled a loose collection of people to share deeply the pain and loneliness experienced in their church and in the world.

On several occasions in the course of this meandering exploration on games we have compared simulation games to parables. We usually think of parables as being a verbal or printed means of conveying a message via a comparison or through a likeness. The stories of Jesus come most readily to mind. These gems of interest and imagination enable us to feel and experience the truth being taught.

ESCAPE. This game was developed in the course of studying the Book of Jonah. We desired a means of knowing experientially the attempt of Jonah to escape his responsibility of going to Nineveh. We drew on the maze idea of the game BLIND which was described earlier.

GAMING

Our goal was to enable the students to act out their options in seeking security in an insecure world. Our tools were common masking tape, sticky-on-both-sides tape, people, and blindfolds for everyone.

We made six or eight circles or "security islands" on the floor of a large basement room with the masking tape. We labeled each "island" with one of the things people use as "security blankets" (i.e., drugs, alcohol, money, family, work, sex, etc.). The enabling team then made complicated routes or traffic patterns from "island" to "island" with ordinary tape. We built in certain "dangerous areas" by using the tape with the double-coated sides. The whole group surveyed the area without blindfolds. Then each person was blindfolded and turned around several times. We started each player at a different point in the course. The players had to use touch while they crawled along routes from "island" to "island." They had to deal with "danger areas" (sticky tape) and also other players as they encountered them. When the player reached a "security island," he had to choose whether to stay and defend it and possibly share it, or to seek another. When everyone had found a security island, we instructed them to remove their blindfolds. We then discussed the kinds of "security" they had found. Is this what they hoped to achieve in life? What were the dangers on the way? What were the problems once there? Are such islands essential in real life? Our debriefing went on and on. Here is a rough outline of the floor plan we used for this living parable or game:

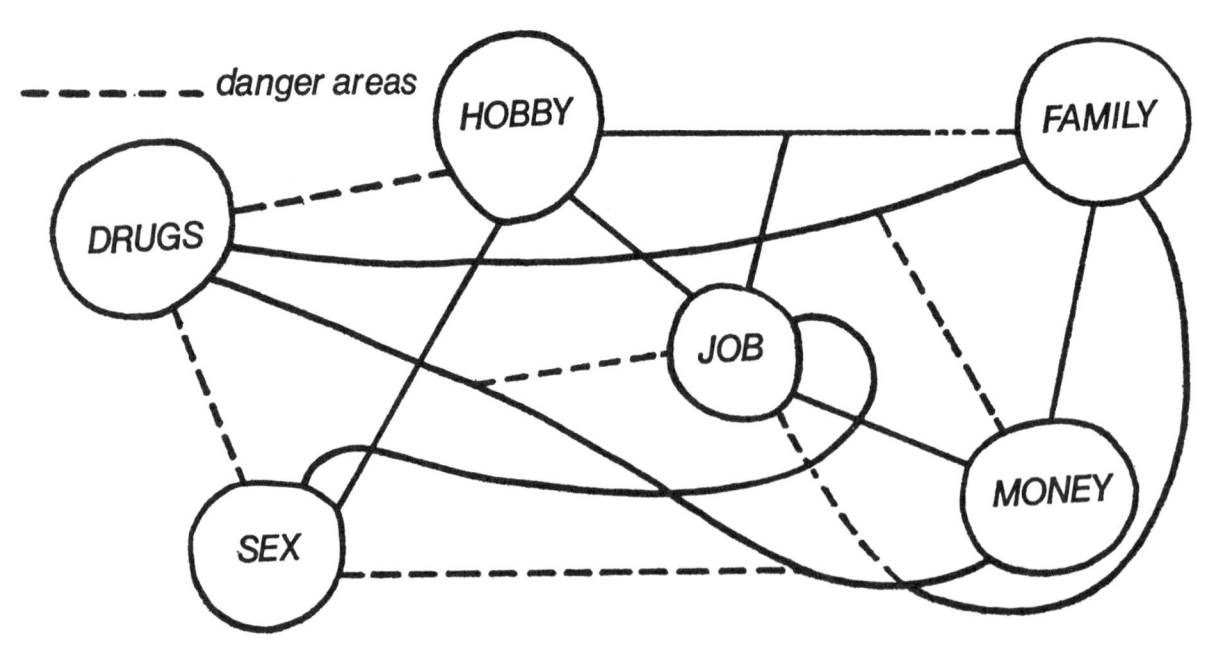

GAMBIT ELEVEN MIND FLINTS

These brief fragments of games are a kind of mind flint. When these and other undigested bits of games are struck against the resources of your people doing a particular task amazing things happen. We must strike sparks of possibilities from each other's ideas. One undigested bit or piece of a teaching probe can be shaped into a fantastic learning event. There is nothing new or unique about the fragments from which games are formed. What is really striking is the unique nurture and actualization that you and your people give to learning experience. This precious step in the teaching/learning process rests in your hands.

Mind flints are to be found in your existing environment. Just let your eyes roam over your book shelf. Numerous games will be suggested by particular books. What could you do with *Games People Play?* Roger Boekenhauer built a whole retreat weekend with games drawn from this book. He had the teenagers playing games like "Wooden Leg" and "If It Weren't for You." The book wasn't written for this purpose. However, Roger utilized a process that I call media recyling to make a series of games for the purpose of learning.

The Peter Principle (Laurence J. Peter and Raymond Hull [New York: Bantam, 1970]) is another book which could act as a mind flint for those interested in gaming as a learning technique. The book leaves you with the uncomfortable conviction that we do indeed rise to the level of our ultimate incompetence. A group of young adults climbing the organizational ladder could well use a game created by you to work out their positions concerning the Christian's role in structured patterns. The book might be reduced to a card-drawing process. The situation could be their job in a mythical company. The stakes could be escalated to deal with some important decisions. What role does the Christian understanding of vocation and personal worth have to play in the positions taken by those in the game?

Even a controversial bestseller like *Everything You Always Wanted to Know about Sex (But Were Afraid to Ask)* (David Reuben [New York: McKay, 1969]) might be a mind flint for you and your young married couples. This group is often neglected by the faith community. We usually wait for them to fit into the older adult pattern. However, there are a number of pressing problems which need to be faced by these folk. The faith community should exercise its responsibility by dealing with the areas of their concern. This bestseller just deals with one small aspect of the broader area of sexuality. However, by making a game out of the book you might find the areas of real concern and provide some theological input for them. Perhaps you and your folk will want to recycle this book as a panel show. Members of the group will be cast in the roles of "experts" on sexuality. Each person in the game may be given a new identity. They have to answer as their play role dictates. The pieces of paper you give each person will narrowly define their position on the questions that will arise. You then draw the questions from the book. You and your planning folk can design something from this mind flint which meets the particular needs of your people.

You can see that the possibilities are endless in this kind of mindset about gaming. In fact,

59

GAMING

once you get into this kind of teaching you will find that too many ideas will swarm over you. Your biggest problem will be to sort them out and seek a clear direction.

When one shares these excitements and possibilities, there is always a danger that the game becomes the thing. People easily get overwhelmed by the thrill of doing this kind of teaching. At this time in our religious teaching situation, it may be important to have people fall into this kind of extreme. We need some kind of counterbalance. However, every authentic teaching design must be based on solid goals. We must keep asking ourselves: "What is it that we are trying to learn?" Authentic theology must express itself in creative teaching. This is another tension point which must be faced by each creative teacher. The mind flints and content bid for priority in the enabler's mind. When such a struggle is narrowly drawn, the student is often lost. It is the intermix of mind flint, content, and student that makes for the learning situation. This is particularly important in the realm of gaming.

GAMBIT TWELVE:
PLAYMANSHIP

It is such a leap from paper and sound to your class! However, it is this process of making the word become flesh and experience which makes learning happen. So often people who write make others think that things were too wonderful in all their experiential situations. The reader is led to believe that it is perfection he is viewing from afar. He is encouraged to feel that he could not do things as well as those being reported. This is nonsense. No event is as good or as bad as it seems in later telling. This does not invalidate the experience. It just should make us have more confidence as we risk for people. Games are no different. A box full of materials for a game gives us confidence because this is the old linear form we have known from childhood. Monotony gives us courage. However, learning in the electric environment forces us to break out of all boxes. The young and old are crying for means of learning by which they can be enabled to deal with reality as theological beings.

A remarkable example of what I am talking about was undertaken by my friend Jane Mall. This creative teacher has built upon her twenty-five years of teaching experience to groove totally her ninth grade class. They have reached such a free stage of learning that they can now fully design their own materials. I recently mentioned in a tape to Jane that I have been struck by the common tea bag. I often do this. Something from the trivial environment will hit me as a potential object for media recycling. I had no idea of where this item from our everyday experience would lead. Jane went to her class and said that Dennis had been turned on by a tea bag. He wants to know how we could use it to teach the Good News. They then spent the hour designing a game around a tea bag!

They first recycled the process of changing dry leaves into steaming tea. For them it was like lifeless man becoming a living man of faith. They then built a game. The students broke down the process of tea bag to tea into several steps (hot water, sugar, cream, lemon, etc.). The teams of students were given so many points

61

toward completing the process for every correct answer they could give concerning the questions a living man of faith should know. These questions were drawn from the Bible. The point of this story is not whether the game they created is the best in the world. It may not even be very original. The value of this response was that the students were designing the means of reorganizing their experience into such a form that they could learn. Wow! If Christian education could only reach these high points more than just occasionally.

Perhaps learning games have been so successful because people like to risk when the stakes don't seem to be high. You can win in play even when you have lost. I remember a summer when I was working my way through school by selling automobiles. I was having a hard time closing a deal. I called over our sales manager. Ed had the fantastic capacity of getting a good reading on the character of a person with just one visual sweep. We were hung up on $75.00. I needed the money in order to have the deal approved. However, the man would not agree to pay this additional amount. Ed talked to him for a few minutes. He had made his character analysis. "I'll tell you what. I will toss you for the difference. If your coin is closest to the wall, I will knock off the $75.00. If I win, you'll pay it." The "sport" was grinning from ear to ear. They tossed and Ed won. The man happily paid the difference. He had played a game for his car and had a story to tell.

Games will not save a dying church school. In order to use successfully any particular method of communication or teaching, you have to get a grasp on the kind of process we discussed earlier. An enabling teacher must know the student. He must know himself. The goals must be established and a solid grasp on the content must be accomplished. Then the process of stringing all these strains together becomes the miracle of good teaching. This means that everything is a medium for teaching. The playing or parabolic approach is just one in a sea of limitless possibilities.

Gaming may be particularly important now because life is so void of good play. Leisure time has become work. The ordinary American, usually cannot relax and enjoy the play of vacation. Perhaps by the use of playing in teaching we may be recapturing an important aspect of Christian theology. Celebration of life.

I concur with Arthur Peterson's concern that so much of the gaming being used in education settings is "intense, purposeful—and humorless" (*Media and Methods,* April 1971, p. 55). It is so tempting to beat our players over the head with the seriousness of theological games. Games are such an easy means of bringing reality home. However, I do think that we can probe the means by which games can really be joyous theological play.

In another context I recently suggested that worship should be more playful *(Let It Run* [Richmond: John Knox, 1971]). The reaction was critical from some. They felt that the holy should be treated with respect: seriousness. Some people treat funerals in this way also. However, the Christian is trapped by a message of thanksgiving, joy, promise, and celebration. If the students don't enjoy a game we should question its teaching value. Learning is fun when it is genuine and absorbing. However, most of us have been so trained by our learning experiences, that this is hard to believe.

When we planned some of the games mentioned in this book, there was always lots of fun. Some of the ideas we came up with were sheer madness. We laughed until we cried. We also cried until we laughed. This is good teaching and good learning.

Let's recap the kind of gaming that we have been sharing with you. The process of creating our kind of games seems to fall into a certain pattern.

In the first place, I always start with a planning group. Six or eight people are gathered to design a particular series or single event. It is important that the atmosphere for such group creativity be free and flooded with good vibes. This means that everyone is accepted and encouraged in all kinds of verbal and nonverbal ways to contribute who they are. A good way to get the group functioning in this kind of creative manner is to have them take a reading on the students to be served. How do you find out who a person is? What does he dream or fear? How does he celebrate? The enabling cadre can spend a whole session finding its own way of answering these and other questions about the students.

The next thing which must be done after an understanding of the constituents has been grasped, is for the planners to establish their goals for the event. What is it that they want to accomplish? The more completely you can define these general thrusts the better developed your learning game will be. What is the theological heart of your content? Study may be called for at this point.

Thirdly, the group must enter an unstructured probing period. This is a crucial experience where all ideas are nurtured and accepted. So many people in religious education limit their mental meandering about teaching possibilities. Any wild suggestion should be seriously entertained. Don't worry about immediate application. Don't discard any idea probe or fragment of an idea because it doesn't seem feasible. Practicality and feasibility are the biggest enemies of creativity. There is always a way to reshape even the most extreme idea into a manageable design. Let the minds of the members of the group wander over things from their past which have impressed them. It is my contention that anything a person is impressed by has some value. The purpose of the planning group's sharing of this task is that each member massages the pieces of unformed ideas with his mind and spirit. One flash of an idea soon absorbs the community energy. It will be recast into new forms and belong to everyone. One person's input is transformed into the community's creation.

The fourth step in the planning process comes after a number of probes have been hatched in this fashion. The definite game-shaping work must now take place. You will be amazed how easy it is to mold a game out of any thrust. Children are marvelous at this process. They make games out of two or three words. It is this kind of freedom that your group will be trying to recapture. When a general game has been defined, let the gaps and holes in it remain. Have pairs within the group take

GAMING

task assignments to work on certain aspects of the game planning. For instance, in the game RALPH we went several directions at an early stage. The task assignments were: (1) problems to be presented by RALPH, (2) room preparations, (3) sound and recording equipment, and (4) general facility preparations. Each sub-group came back to the next meeting with ideas on how things should be organized. This new input changed some of the initial ideas developed at the first meeting. Many new ideas were presented at this meeting.

The fifth layer of planning is to tighten up the design carefully. Each facet of the game must be worked out. The leadership of sections of the game must be established. In my work we usually use the planning group as the game masters. They execute what they have designed. There is natural excitement and expectation with those who are doing what they have created.

The final step in the process of creating learning games comes after the actual playing. The group should gather again and debrief what happened in the learning event. This is an important step in creative teaching. The group will have a real closeness and be anxious to share what they each experienced. This is also the best moment to pick up the enthusiasm of their creativity for another application. Such sensitive follow-through can assure long-range impact of your creative experiments. It is the long-term goal of learning which must guide all your exploratory probes into new teaching techniques.

It is quite important to realize that games don't belong to certain persons. Creative germs are always floating around in the environment.

It is acceptable and perhaps necessary that these bits of idea matter be "caught" for particular usage. It may be that creativity is really the process of intermix or cross fertilization. In fact, many of the gaming ideas in this book have been around for hundreds of years. However, what makes something a medium for learning is that it takes living flesh and touches your students. Only you and your people can make ideas and teaching approaches into vivid learning experiences.

Gaming then is a slippery means by which good learning can take place. This technique is not new or unusual to good teaching. In fact it is closely akin to several other good methods.

We have been sharing a "folk" approach to simulation games. These games are developed by ordinary people in every case. These games are not designed to compete with the scientific games which are tested by computors. The games shared here can be done by anyone. They can be changed and twisted into new shapes to fit given situations and given people. Everybody is playing with gaming. You have to try it.

Go back now and play Record I, Side 1, Bands I and II. What does this suggest to you concerning your teaching situation? Play with all this print and sound experience. Share with me how it goes with you (Abingdon Press, 201 8th Avenue South, Nashville, Tennessee 37302). I am anxious to celebrate the unique creativity you and your folk bring to the process of seeking the truth. There is much untouched opportunity in the creation of your games, brothers and sisters. Shake it loose. Your God will enable you to play, to learn, and to enjoy it!